# Ourselves
# Stages 1 & 2

A Unit for teachers

Published for the Schools Council by
Macdonald Educational, London and Milwaukee

First published in Great Britain 1973 by
**Macdonald Educational Ltd**
Holywell House, Worship Street
London EC2A 2EN

Macdonald-Raintree Inc.
205 W. Highland Avenue
Milwaukee, Wisconsin 53203

Reprinted 1974, 1976 (with amendments), 1977, 1978,
1980, 1981

ISBN 0 356 04349 5

Library of Congress Catalog Card Number
77-83006

The chief author of this book is:

Roy Richards

The other members of the Science 5/13 team are:

| | |
|---|---|
| Len Ennever | Project Director |
| Albert James | Deputy Project Director |
| Wynne Harlen | Evaluator |
| Sheila Parker | |
| Don Radford | |
| Mary Horn | |

Made and printed by Waterlow (Dunstable) Limited

# General preface

'Science 5/13' is a Project sponsored jointly by the Schools Council, the Nuffield Foundation and the Scottish Education Department, and based at the University of Bristol School of Education. It aims at helping teachers to help children between the ages of five and thirteen years to learn science through first-hand experience using a variety of methods.

The Project produces books that comprise Units dealing with subject areas in which children are likely to conduct investigations. Some of these Units are supported by books of background information.
The Units are linked by objectives that the Project team hopes children will attain through their work. The aims of the Project are explained in a general guide for teachers called, *With objectives in mind,* which contains the Project's guide to Objectives for children learning science, reprinted at the back of each Unit.

## Acknowledgements

The Project is deeply grateful to its many friends:
to the local education authorities who have helped
us work in their areas, to those of their staff who, acting
as area representatives, have borne the heavy brunt of
administering our trials, and to the teachers, heads and
wardens who have been generous without stint in
working with their children on our materials. The books
we have written drew substance from the work they
did for us, and it was through their critical appraisal
that our materials reached their present form. For
guidance, we had our sponsors, our Consultative
Committee and, for support, in all our working, the
University of Bristol. To all of them we acknowledge
our many debts: their help has been invaluable.

## Metrication

This has given us a great deal to think about. We have
been given much good advice by well-informed friends,
and we have consulted many reports by learned bodies.
Following the advice and the reports wherever possible
we have expressed quantities in metric units with
Imperial units afterwards in square brackets if it seemed
useful to state them so.

There are, however, some cases to which the
recommendations are difficult to apply. For instance we
have difficulty with units such as miles per hour (which
has statutory force in this country) and with some
Imperial units that are still in current use for common
commodities and, as far as we know, liable to remain
so for some time. In these cases we have tried to use
our common sense, and, in order to make statements
that are both accurate and helpful to teachers we have
quoted Imperial measures followed by the approximate
metric equivalent in square brackets if it seemed
sensible to give them.

Where we have quoted statements made by children,
or given illustrations that are children's work, we have
left unaltered the units in which the children worked
—in any case some of these units were arbitrary.

# Contents

# Introduction

Why a text on 'Ourselves'? There are *three main reasons:*

## We should know something about ourselves

Robert Boyle once said that it is 'highly dishonourable for a Reasonable Soul to live in so Divinely built a Mansion as the Body she resides in, altogether unacquainted with the exquisite structure of it'.

Finding out things about the body *for oneself* is more interesting, rewarding and fun than reading about them in books. Consequently the whole emphasis of this Unit is on aspects of ourselves that can be discovered at first hand.

## Children are interested in themselves

Children are always interested in themselves: in their weight, height, eye colour; in whether someone has his first toe longer than his big toe, in who has the longest legs, in who can do something more quickly, more skilfully than others.

In order to satisfy this interest they will have to question one another, take measurements, get one another to perform certain tasks, carry out tests, record information and make their findings intelligible to others.

## Children will gain an understanding of biological variation

Like begets like and yet we are all so different. Eye colour, hair colour, fingerprints, shape of ears, specific differences show up clearly. The idea of variation will emerge, a useful idea because modern theories of evolution can be built on it as a child gets older.

'Ourselves' is a topic with many facets, and a number of the activities suggested can be linked up with simple and undisturbing issues of health.

Common sense is needed in tackling some of the activities. For example it is wise to know something of a child's pedigree when considering eye colour, adopted children could be 'hurt'. Common sense and caution are also needed when dealing with aspects like memory and flat feet. Safety factors are important, leaping about or blowing into a bell-jar to measure the capacity of the lungs will need to be carefully supervised. For a number of the activities it is wise to ensure that all children taking part are physically fit. There are also moral issues that can be usefully discussed such as the 'ethics' of taking fingerprints.

# Where do we begin?

There is no one place to begin. Generally speaking, the best work comes from spontaneous interest and questioning by children.

It might be of interest to list some of the starting points that have arisen during trials of *Ourselves* in schools:

From one girl's father being a policeman. This led to a visit to a police station to see how fingerprints were taken.

From beginning with how many boys and how many girls were in the class.

From a teacher bringing his newly born daughter to school for regular recordings of her length, weight, diet and behaviour.

From an interest in footwear leading to an examination of feet.

From a television programme on Eskimos. This led to considering how we were like and yet different from them.

From a project on metric units leading to measuring the body.

From one girl in the class having eyes of different colour.

From a class discussion about themselves. Beginning with their likes and dislikes.

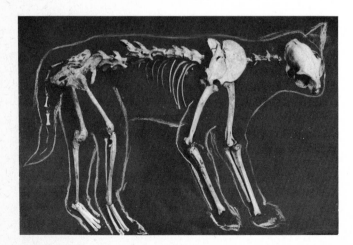

Last sunday 27th FeBruary 1972 Me and Mark was playing Bows and Arrows Mark fired an Arrow and it went into Some Bushes we went into the Bushes to have a look Then Mark called out come over here. when I came over I saw a skeleton of a cat Then me and Mark found an old Tin Box so we put The Bones into The Box and took it Down Marks house and put it in Germ killer then we Brout it to school.

TiM LiNES

2

Such starting points invariably lead to investigations of a wide general nature. This is as it should be and is to be encouraged.

Here is one case history, set out as a flow chart, to illustrate how this happens. The children even tackled putting a cat's skeleton together.

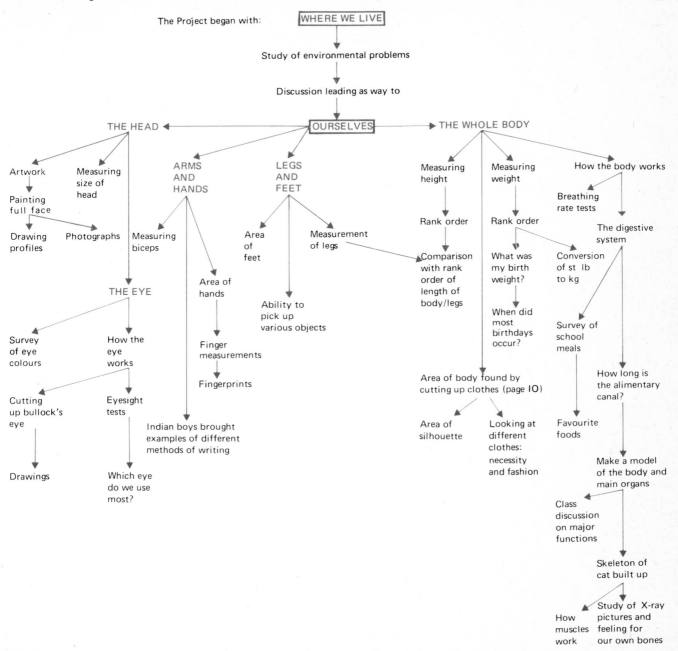

The Project began with: WHERE WE LIVE

Study of environmental problems

Discussion leading as way to

OURSELVES

THE HEAD

THE WHOLE BODY

Artwork

Measuring size of head

ARMS AND HANDS

LEGS AND FEET

Measuring height

Measuring weight

How the body works

Painting full face

Breathing rate tests

Drawing profiles

Photographs

Measuring biceps

Area of feet

Measurement of legs

Rank order

Rank order

The digestive system

Comparison with rank order of length of body/legs

What was my birth weight?

Conversion of st lb to kg

THE EYE

Area of hands

Survey of school meals

Ability to pick up various objects

When did most birthdays occur?

How long is the alimentary canal?

Survey of eye colours

How the eye works

Finger measurements

Area of body found by cutting up clothes (page 10)

Favourite foods

Cutting up bullock's eye

Eyesight tests

Fingerprints

Area of silhouette

Looking at different clothes: necessity and fashion

Make a model of the body and main organs

Indian boys brought examples of different methods of writing

Class discussion on major functions

Drawings

Which eye do we use most?

Skeleton of cat built up

How muscles work

Study of X-ray pictures and feeling for our own bones

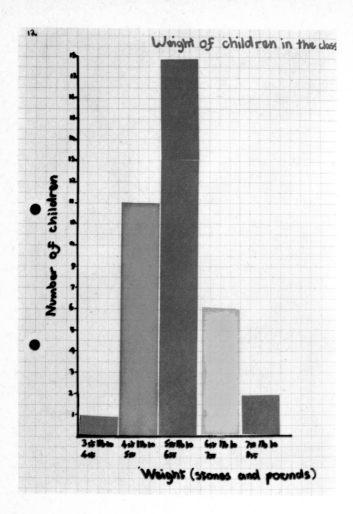

Weight of children in the class

Number of children

Weight (stones and pounds)

3 st 11b to 4 st | 4 st 11b to 5 st | 5 st 11b to 6 st | 6 st 11b to 7 st | 7 st 11b to 8 st

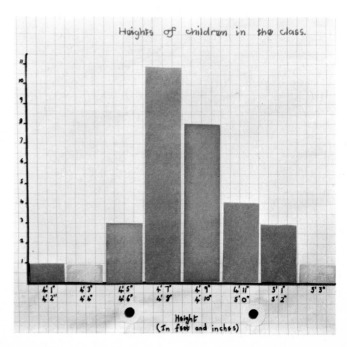

Heights of children in the class.

Height
(In feet and inches)

4' 1" 4' 2" | 4' 3" 4' 4" | 4' 5" 4' 6" | 4' 7" 4' 8" | 4' 9" 4' 10" | 4' 11" 5' 0" | 5' 1" 5' 2" | 5' 3"

# All of us

Start by looking at the body as a whole.

## How tall are you?

Mark out a centimetre scale on the door surround to just above the height of the largest person in the class. Measure the height of children in the class and make a record.

What is the commonest height in the class?

How many very short children are there?

How many very tall children are there?

Encourage the shortest and the tallest children in the class to measure their parents. Do very short children tend to have very short parents? Do very tall children tend to have very tall parents?

Graph heights of boys and girls separately. Do these graphs show a difference?

### Height sitting
Measure the height of people *sitting*.

Make sure they all use the same chair!

Can you tell from your results which children are long-legged?

## How heavy are you?

Weigh yourself. Record the result.

Guess the weight of other children in the class. How right were you? Do you get better with practice? Make a record of your results.

Is there any correlation between height and weight?

Can you improvise a method of finding the weight of a child if you have only kitchen scales?

## What area does your silhouette cover?

Ask a friend to lie down on squared paper and draw round him. Count up the squares to obtain his area. There are bound to be some incomplete squares. Count those incomplete squares whose area is greater than fifty per cent and neglect those below this size.

## How much skin do you have?

How would you find out the general body surface area? You could skin someone as was suggested by one nine-year-old but here are three separate humane ways of finding an answer which have come from three different junior schools.

Mainly:

By measuring the silhouette on squared paper.

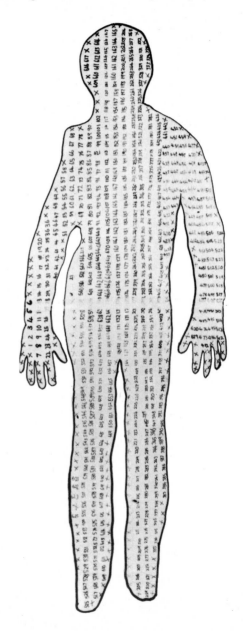

Area of the Body.

First we got some squared paper and Sellotaped it together and then we drew round Peter Hearn. We counted the whole squares and put crosses in all the half or more squares. We left out the parts wich were less than half a square. There were 534 full squares, and 155 portions of one half or more. This makes a total of 689 complete squares. Each square is four square centimetres. So the total number of square centimetres is 689 × 4 = 2756 sq cm. Our diagram represents only one front (or back) of the body and so to obtain the total area of the body we shall require 2 × 2756 which is 5512.
We still have not allowed for the sides of the body. We estimated that two sides of the body would be roughly equal to one front (or back) so we added another 2756 sq cm. = 5512 + 2756 = 8268 sq cm.

By cutting cylinders of squared paper to fit the limbs.

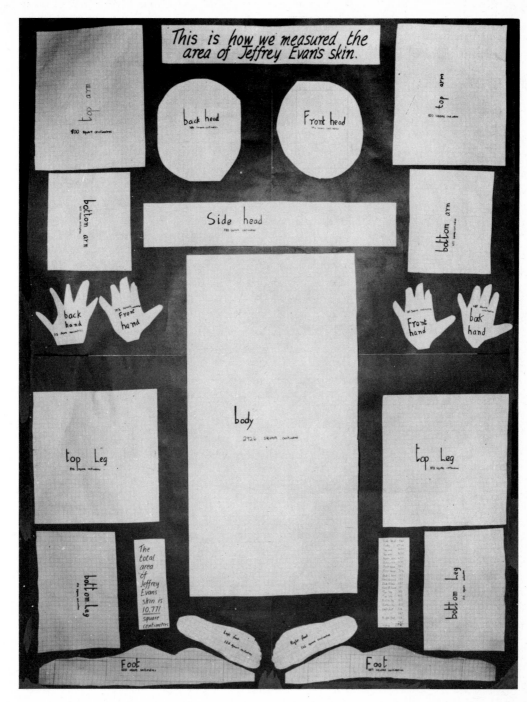

This is how we measured the area of Jeffrey Evan's skin.

Continued
on page 10

7

This is how some
six-year-olds
classified faces

Can you paint
with a brush
held by your
toes? This is
a five-year-
old's attempt

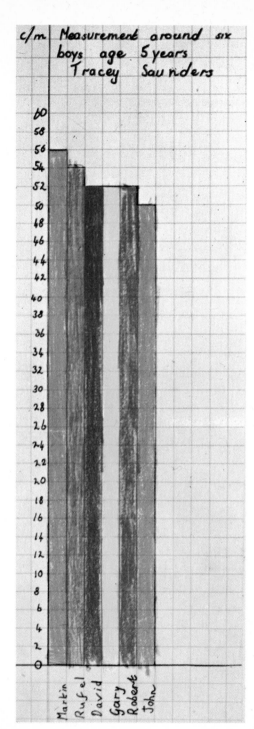

c/m Measurement around six boys age 5 years
Tracey Saunders

Martin Rufel David Gary Robert John

Maria Vincent.
Measurement around six girls heads age 5 years.
c/m

Karen Maxine Julie Yvette Sarah Claire

See the section on measuring heads on page 11

By working out the area covered by garments.

A very patient piece of work was carried out by a girl of eleven with the reading age of a six-year-old. She became very engrossed in the task and worked away at it for different times over a period of a month. Not only did she carefully work out the area covered by her clothes but painstakingly worked out the area covered by her hands using Plasticine.

Volume might be interesting too. How about some homework in the bath! (Under parental supervision.)

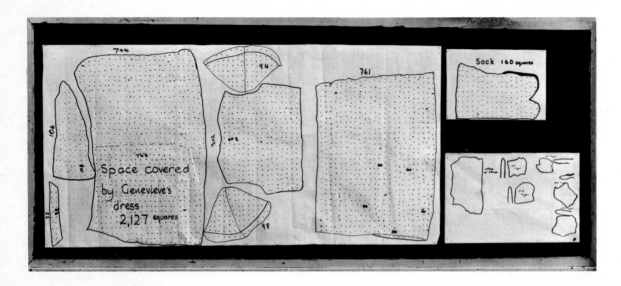

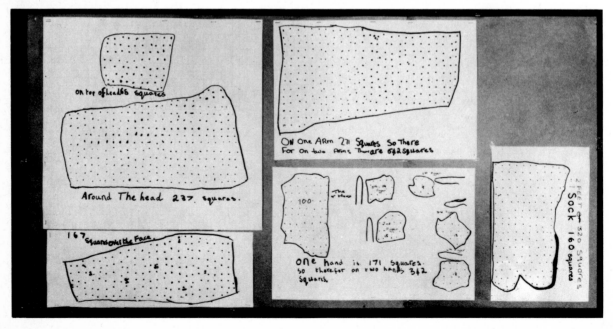

# Heads and faces

## Head shapes and sizes

Heads are different shapes. There should be an intriguing variety in any class. How many children have a double crown? How many can feel bumps?

### Faces
Look closely at the faces of some of your friends. Do any two of them have the same shape nose? List all the ways in which the faces differ.

Draw some profiles and some full-face views of your friends. Try them out on members of the class. Can they tell who is who? You can often get good silhouettes in the beam of light from a projector. These are relatively easy to draw round. Can you classify the shapes of faces in your class? How many are:

round
oval
square
oblong
heart-shaped? (See page 8).

Collect baby pictures of children in the class. In which ways have the faces changed?

### Measuring heads
Try measuring heads with a tape-measure.

Make sure you measure each head in the same region; just above the eyebrows for example.

If possible take a random sample of head sizes of the youngest and oldest children in the school. What conclusions do you reach?

Make a collection of baby pictures. What strikes you about the head size in relation to the total body size?

Here is some children's writing that goes with the graphs on page 9.

> Do Our Heads Grow with our bodies?
> Maria Vincent.
>
> My friend and I went to the youngest infants class-room and we measured around the heads of six boys and six girls. We made two graphs one for the boys and one for the girls.
> The next day we went to the top junior class-room and we did the same thing. We made two more graphs.
> We found the averages.
> The average 5 year old girl had a head measurement of 53cm.
> The average 5 year old boy had a head measurement of 53cm.
> The average 10 year old girl had a head measurement of 54cm.
> The five year old boys had slightly bigger heads than the 5 year old girls.
> The 10 year old girls had slightly bigger heads than the 10 year old boys.
> Babies heads are big in comparison with the body.

## Eyes and looking

### An eye survey
Count the eyes of each colour in the class and make a chart to indicate the distribution.

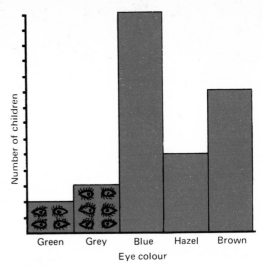

Number of children

Green  Grey  Blue  Hazel  Brown
Eye colour

### Eye colour
Each individual possesses two genes (hereditary factors) for any particular trait, be it eye colour, hair colour, shape of nose or long eyelashes. A child will inherit *one* gene for each particular trait from each of its parents. These genes will determine the child's final appearance.

Genes do not blend together to determine what particular traits appear. What happens is that some genes are more forceful than others and 'dominate' their opposite number. Dark eyes are 'dominant' to light eyes, for example. The gene for light eyes is thus said to be 'recessive'.

If one gene is dominant and the other recessive in any one parent then the odds on which genes turn up in the offspring are easy to calculate. It is just like tossing two coins many times. On average you would get both heads one in four times, both tails one in four times and heads and tails together two in four times.

If heads represent the dominant gene for eye colour (D for dark eyes), then there are three chances out of four of it appearing in any resultant offspring because heads turns up three out of four tosses.

Let us take a look at the odds at work as far as eye colour is concerned remembering that dark eyes are dominant to light eyes.

### All dark eyes on one side of the family

This will result in almost all children being dark eyed no matter what colour the eyes of the partner.

D = dark-eyed                     d = light-eyed

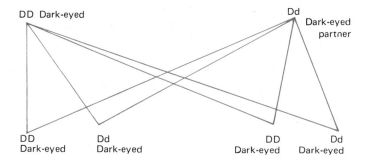

### Both parents dark-eyed but with light-eyed relatives

Here the odds are 3:1 that children will be dark-eyed.

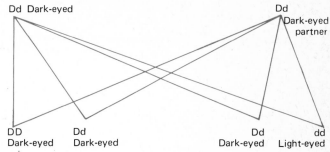

### One dark-eyed parent with light-eyed relatives; the other parent light-eyed

Here there is a 50:50 chance of children being dark-eyed.

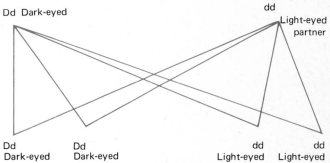

### Both parents light-eyed

Here the offspring will almost always be light-eyed.

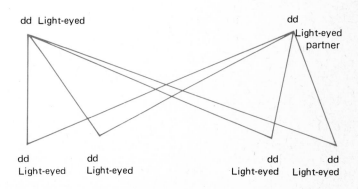

All this may seem a little complex but will help to explain the results as they were set out by children in one school.

| Grandparents | | Colour of grandparents eyes | Parents | Colour of Parents eyes | Child | Colour of child's eyes |
|---|---|---|---|---|---|---|
| Grandmother } MILLS Grandfather | | Light Light | Father MILLS | Light | Rebecca Mills | Dark |
| Grand mother } THOMAS Grand Father | | Dark Light | Mother MILLS | Dark | | |
| Grandmother } SYKES Grandfather | | Light Light | Father SYKES | Light | Fiona SYKES | Light |
| Grandmother } BARRY Grandfather | | Light Light | Mother SYKES | Light | | |
| Grand Mother } BRACEY Grand Father | | Dark Light | Father BRACEY | Dark | Susan Bracey | Light |
| Grand mother } RANDALL Grand Father | | Dark Light | Mother Bracey | Light | | |
| Grandmother } TARZEY Grandfather | | Dark Light | Father TARZEY | Dark | Robert Tarzey | Dark |
| Grand Mother } MOOR Grand Father | | Dark Light | Mother TARZEY | Dark | | |
| Grandmother } BURNS COX Grand father | | Light Dark | Father BURNS COX | Light | Simon Burns Cox | Light |
| Grand Mother } STEVENSON Grand father | | Light Dark | Mother BURNS COX | Light | | |

Paula Hollingsworth

*Eye colour relationship from grandparents*

*to child*

We have started an investigation about the colour of eyes. We asked people to bring in a chart showing the colour of their grandparents, their parents and their colour. We separated them into groups. We called grey, grey-blue, bue and green - LIGH and hazel and brown - DARK.

In the Mills family the child has taken the colour of eyes from the mother not the father. In the Sykes family everybody is light coloured. The Tarzey family has only two grandparents with dark eyes but the parents and child dark eyes. Really we need moore children but so far I think that dark is stronger than light.

## How well can you see?

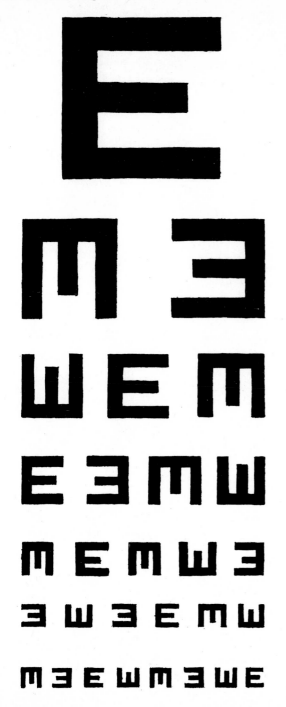

This is the sort of eye chart that is used to test the eyes of children who cannot read letters accurately.

Cut out a cardboard 'E'.

Ask a partner to sit about 3 metres away from the chart and cover one eye.

Give him the cut-out and ask him to move it to the same position as the one you indicate on the chart.

A child with normal vision should be able to do this right down to the bottom line.

Form a group of four or five children.

Who can see the furthest? Perhaps the chart will help you to find out.

Better still you might invent your own tests for finding an answer.

Don't forget to test right and left eyes separately as well as both eyes together.

Such an exercise is a good time to discuss eye care. Why should we sit in a good light and avoid glare, not hold a book too near the face, not sit in a room lit just by television or rub our eyes with dirty hands?

### Fun with eyes
**Which eye do you use most?**
Line up a pencil with the edge of a window or a door frame keeping both eyes open.

Close your right eye! Open it!

Now close your left eye.

Usually the pencil jumps sharply to one side when one of the eyes is closed. This is the eye that was used to line up the pencil, and the eye that is used most.

How many children have right eyes that are dominant?

How many children have left eyes that are dominant?

Are left-eyed people left-handed?

### Finding your range of vision

Hold a pencil at arm's length in front of you. Without moving your head or eyes, move the pencil sideways until it goes out of sight.

Try it to the right and to the left.

Repeat the exercise with the pencil above and below your eye level.

Do it all over again, this time moving your eyes but not your head.

### Why two eyes?

Get a partner to hold a pencil, point uppermost, at various distances in front of you.

Keeping *both* eyes open try to touch the point of your partner's pencil with a pencil of your own.

Try with right eye closed.

Try with left eye closed.

When was it easiest? Can you explain why?

Hold out the bottom end of your fountain pen at arm's length. With *both* eyes open, lower the top on to it. How easy is it?

Close your right eye. Starting with the top of your pen held above your head bring it forward and lower it on to the pen.

Now close your left eye and repeat the operation. How easy is it with one eye closed?

Put two toy cars in line with one another. Try to get a third car in line with the others by towing it with a piece of thread.

Try using both eyes and then each eye in turn.

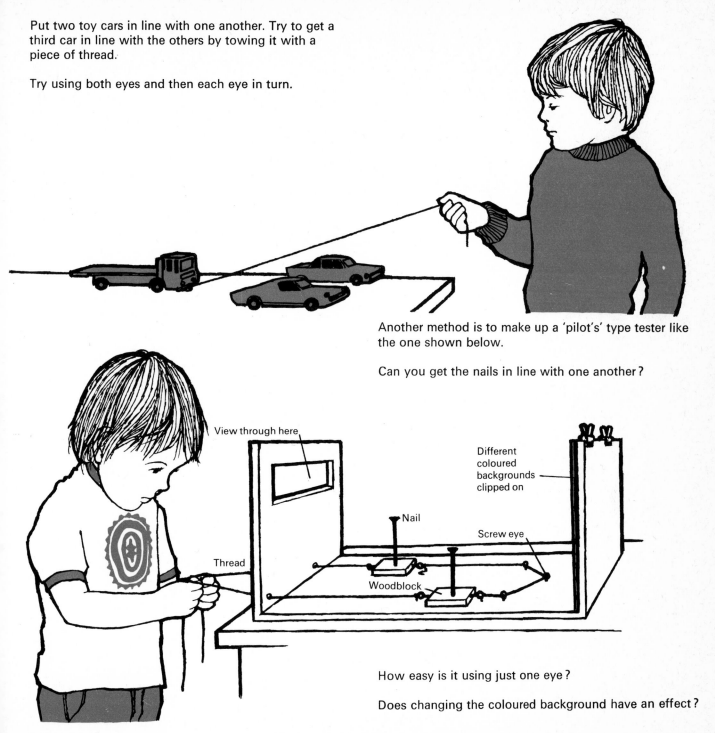

Another method is to make up a 'pilot's' type tester like the one shown below.

Can you get the nails in line with one another?

View through here

Different coloured backgrounds clipped on

Nail

Screw eye

Thread

Woodblock

How easy is it using just one eye?

Does changing the coloured background have an effect?

## What does the pupil do?

Stand a friend facing a window. Look at the pupils of
his eyes. Ask him to keep his eyes open but shut them
off from the light for ten seconds by covering them
with his hands.

Now let him uncover his eyes. Do the pupils change?
Can you think of a reason why they should?

Which of these two drawings shows the pupil in
bright light?

Even with very young children the acuteness of observation that comes from first-hand experience can be
startling. On the right is a splendid piece of recording by
a six-year-old about looking at the pupil.

## Finding the 'blindspot'

The area of the eye that receives light rays when they
have passed through the pupil is called the retina.
It is covered with light-sensitive cells except for a small
region where the optic nerve leaves its surface for the
brain. This region is consequently called the 'blindspot'
and is insensitive to light rays. This can be demonstrated
in the following way.

**X**

Move the page away from the right eye with the left
eye closed. If you look fixedly at the X, the black spot
will seem to disappear. Light rays from this region are
falling on the blindspot.

A pupil is a little sort of window in your eye it lets the light into your eyes so that you can see everything it is like a little camera when you stand in the light your pupil gets smaller because you don't need so much light When you stand in the dark your pupil gets bigger because you need more light When I looked into Pauls eyes they were brown with his pupil in the middle there were little red things in the white of his eye he has big twinkling eyes I could see the windows and myself reflected in his eyes he has long black eyelashes.

## A mirage

Hold both your forefingers nail to nail about 6 cm in front of your eyes.

Look at an imaginary point in the distance beyond them. Do not look directly at the fingers.

Now separate your fingertips slowly. What do you see?

## Seeing through your hand

Roll up some card to make a tube. Look through the tube at any distant object.

Cover your other eye with the palm of your hand, but keep your eyes open. Slowly move your hand away from your eye along the side of the tube.

What do you see? Why is this?

## Persistence of vision

Draw a goldfish on one side of a piece of card and a goldfish bowl on the other, *directly* behind it.

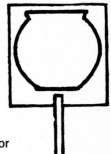

Sellotape the card to a pencil or insert it into the split end of a cane, and spin it in your hands.

What happens?

What happens if you vary the speed that you spin the card?

## Recognising colour

Take a coloured object. Ask a friend to sit comfortably and gaze straight ahead. Slowly move the coloured object into his range of vision.

Where does he first *see* the object?

Where does he first recognise its colour?

Try a range of colours. Test a number of people. Which colours show up best? What about colour on *different backgrounds?*

Compare white letters on a black background with purple letters on a black background. Which colour combinations would be good to use for signs? Go for a walk and record which colours and combinations of colours predominate in advertisements and road signs.

## What is the greatest distance at which you can make out black dots?

Mark up a series of white cards with black dots at their centre.

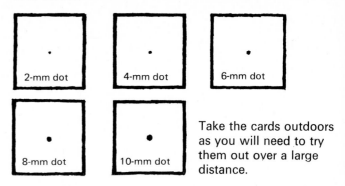

Take the cards outdoors as you will need to try them out over a large distance.

One child shows the marked side and the plain white side of each card in turn to a partner. The partner advances until he can just make out the dot. What sort of results do you get for a group of children?

## What colours suit you best?

| | Red | | Orange | | Yellow | | Green | | Brown | | Violet | |
|---|---|---|---|---|---|---|---|---|---|---|---|---|
| | Yes | No | Yes | No | Yes | No | Yes | No | Yes | No | Yes | No |
| Tony | ////// | / | ///// | // | / | /////// | etc. | | | | | |
| Jean | | | | | | | | | | | | |
| Ann | | | | | | | | | | | | |
| John | | | | | | | | | | | | |
| etc. | | | | | | | | | | | | |

What colour combinations would suit each of the figures on page 20?

What do your friends think of your choices?

Get your friends to vote on which colours they think suit you best. Which colours do they think suit other members of your group? Record the number of votes in a chart as shown at the top of this page.

Check on the votes by holding large squares of coloured paper in front of each child to see if the colour really does suit him or not.

## Optical illusions
There are many things that 'trick' the eye. Two are shown below, a third top right.

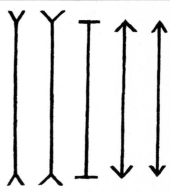

Which line is longest?

Many optical illusions can be drawn on card and clear plastic so that the conflicting information can be removed and the answer seen.

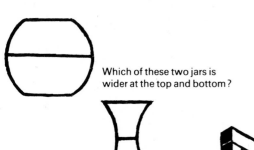

Which of these two jars is wider at the top and bottom?

Is this possible?
Try to trace the sides
of the triangle

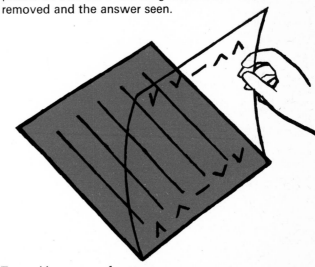

Try making some of your own.

## How far can you walk in a straight line blindfolded?

Walk in a straight line across the playground. Get a friend to record your pathway with chalk.

Begin at the same starting point but this time blindfold yourself. What is the record of your progress like this time? Are boys better than girls in judging how straight a line they can walk?

## Ears and hearing

### Ear lobes
Another dominant character, like dark eye colour, is free ear lobes. Fixed ear lobes being recessive.

How many children have these sort of ear lobes?

How many children have ear lobes like these?

Check back through parents and grandparents to see what sort of ear lobes they possess.

### Direction of sounds
Choose a quiet area with plenty of space.

Blindfold a friend and sit him comfortably in a chair. Make sure that he keeps his head pointing directly forward.

Ring a bell directly in front of him at about his chest level.

Can he point to the bell?

Try ringing the bell in other positions—to his right, to his left, behind, above and below him. Record the correct guesses and measure their direction from the chair.

Try this for a large number of children and make a graph of the sound direction plotted against number of children who successfully guessed it.

Usually sounds from the sides are easily located, sounds from the front and rear and overhead are more difficult to locate. This is not surprising since the eyes cover ground in front of us and our ears cover ground to the sides. The two senses work together and are complementary.

Try the experiment with ringing the bell all over again but this time cover up one ear. Is the right ear better than the left ear at judging the direction of sounds?

Make some trumpet-like ears from card.

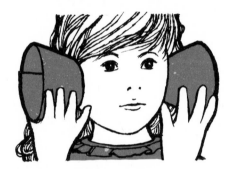

Does directional hearing improve?

Does the distance over which one can hear improve?

## Guessing sounds

Blindfold one of your friends. Drop various objects such as coins, a rubber, a penknife, a comb and so on on to the table. Can your friend name the objects from the sound?

Drop a range of coins. Can he tell what each coin is? Does he get better with practice?

Record a number of sounds on the tape-recorder— footsteps, pouring water, drawing a finger along the teeth of a comb, rubbing two pieces of sandpaper together, blowing down a drinking straw into water and so on. Can other people guess the sounds when they are replayed? Try turning the volume control up. What effect does it have on the guesses?

Can you guess your friends' voices? Sit blindfolded and try and recognise each of your friends as they repeat a sentence in their normal voice. Try making sounds behind a screen. Can your friends guess them?

## Echoes

You will need a very quiet room to do this. Move all desks and chairs away and make a large clear area.

Blindfold a child and ask him to walk towards the wall.

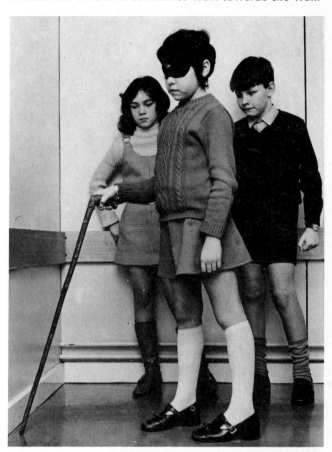

How close can he get without touching it? *Tell him to listen to his footsteps.*

Try other children. How close can they get?

Now repeat the game but this time use a walking stick to tap in front of you. Does the sound it makes help?

# How good is your hearing?

Can you hear a pin drop? How near do you have to be? Does it matter what you drop it on or from how high you drop it? Does it matter which way you face?

Form a group of six or seven children. Can you put yourselves in order of hearing ability? Discuss how to do it. You'll probably find that you need a quiet area and some source of sound that is constant and fairly quiet.

How are you going to find out if each of your ears is equally good?

## Fun with listening
### Singing in a bucket

Put your head into a clean metallic bucket and speak. What does it sound like?

Try singing.

What is happening to the sound in the bucket?

### Listening to your watch

Find a watch with a 'soft' tick. Stuff your ears with cotton wool. Hold the watch so that it firmly touches your forehead.

Can you still hear the ticking? Why should this happen?

Put your watch on the desk alongside you. Can you hear it?

Hold a ruler or a piece of wood so that one end touches the watch and the other rests gently against your ear.

Can you still hear the watch?

When is it easiest to hear the watch. What does this tell you?

It is sometimes easier to put a piece of dowelling or metal rod into a plastic funnel. This can then be placed comfortably over the ear.

Funnel        Rod

## What is in the tin?

Get a number of clean, empty coffee tins. Put a different object or substance in each one. For example you might try a pin, sand, sugar, treacle, a match-stick, a rubber, Plasticine, a piece of chalk, a marble, a button, a drawing-pin and so on.

Ask someone to try and guess what is in each tin by the *sound* made as they move the tin about in their hand. Try it with a lot of children. Make a record of the results.

## Hair

Hair types vary enormously but generally speaking curly or wavy hair is dominant. Dark hair tends to be dominant and light hair recessive (see page 13).

How many different hair types can you find in your class? . . . in your school?

Take a snippet of each type from a willing victim and mount them with a piece of Sellotape.

Can you find any way of grouping the hair types?

Can you devise a key to classify the hair found in your school?

If you have a micrometer you can measure the width of hairs. Is curly hair thicker than straight hair?

## Strength of hair

Collect some long hairs to try this. You'll probably need to make up a hair testing device to carry out tests with any accuracy.

Try different coloured hairs: brunette/blonde/auburn/grey/black.

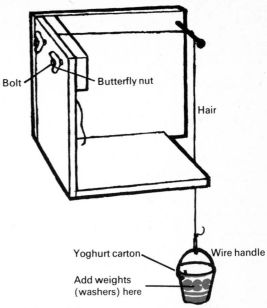
Bolt    Butterfly nut    Hair    Yoghurt carton    Wire handle    Add weights (washers) here

Try hair from different ages, sexes, races.

Is bleached hair stronger than unbleached hair?

## Hair and eye colour

Is there a link between hair and eye colour? Try listing members of the class under headings:

Dark hair with dark eyes.      Dark hair with light eyes.

Light hair with light eyes.      Light hair with dark eyes.

Which combination predominates?

Can you try more complex relationships. Try listing children under the following headings:

| Name | Colour of | | | Type of hair |
|------|------|------|------|------|
|  | Skin | Eyes | Hair |  |
|  |  |  |  |  |

How many children have exactly the same combinations of skin colour, eye colour, hair colour and type of hair?

## Noses and smelling

A Roman nose, that is a nose with a high bridge, is genetically dominant over a straight nose. If parents tend to have broad, prominent or long noses these are passed on to their offspring. Have a look at the nose types in the class.

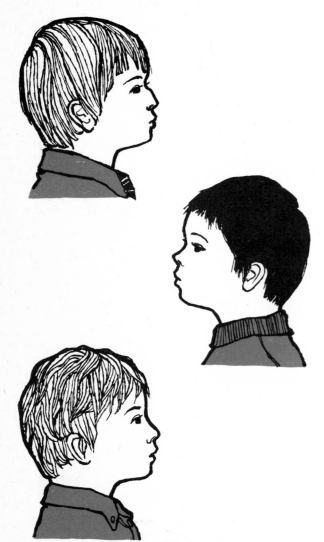

How many broad or prominent noses are there?

## How good a sense of smell have you?

Collect a number of small pots. Those tiny plastic pots that hold jam or empty meat-paste jars will do. Wash them thoroughly and dry them.

Put a series of substances with a distinctive smell in each of the containers, for example: vinegar, tea, chopped grass, perfume, coffee, mothballs, fish, shoe polish, apple, banana, cheese and so on. Cover the tops with muslin. If necessary put black paper around the outside of the jar so that the contents cannot be seen.

Can you guess what is in each container by smell alone?

Test other people. How do they get on? Make a block graph to illustrate your results.

Try liquids alone. Vinegar, cooking oil, turpentine, paraffin, shampoo, some disinfectants, cordials, orange and lemon squash, Pepsi-Cola, Coca-Cola.

**Be very careful**—only use one or two drops in each container and *never* use ammonia or things such as Harpic, petrol or dry-cleaning fluid.

# Mouths

## Tongues and speaking
### Tongue rolling and folding
Tongues vary in length. Some people can even touch their nose with their tongue.

A trait that is passed on from parent to offspring is the ability to fold or roll the tongue.

Some people can do both these things, some can only do one and some can do neither.

How many children can fold their tongue like this?

### Speaking
Stand in front of a large mirror. Watch your face carefully as you say the alphabet.

What things do you use to speak?

Do the same things need to be moved to say each letter?

What happens to your tongue when you talk?

Keep your tongue still but try to talk. What happens?

Stick your tongue out and let it hang loosely. Now speak. What happens?

Hold your tongue and try talking to your neighbour.

Can you find any words that can be spoken without moving your tongue?

## Teeth and eating
Count the number of teeth in your mouth.

Do your friends have the same number?

Make a survey throughout the school.

Number of teeth per person in the nursery (3–5 years)
infants (5–7 years)
juniors (7–11 years)

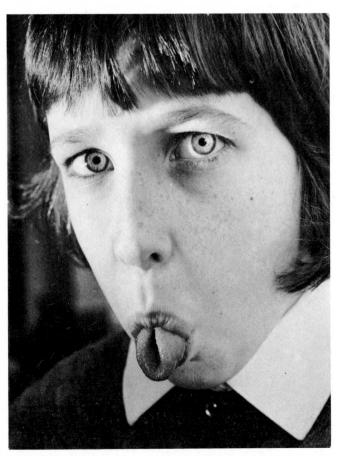

How many children can roll their tongue like this?

Are these teeth all the same? What sort of differences can you find? Examine your own teeth closely in a mirror.

Make a record of your teeth as they are at the moment.

Draw two semi-circles. Make 16 spaces in each semicircle as shown. One space for each tooth.

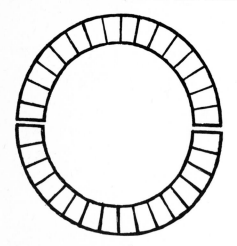

Mark in where a tooth is alright, where a tooth has been extracted, where there are any fillings, where there is a cavity and where a tooth has not yet appeared.

### Which is the best way of cleaning teeth?
Is it best to clean teeth: up and down, across, both up and down and across, not at all?

Try eating a chocolate biscuit and then clean your teeth by each of the methods in turn. Which is best?

Get other children to try the test. What things do you need to standardise to make the test as 'fair' as possible?

Should all children eat the biscuit in the same way with the same number of jaw motions?

Should they all give the same number of brush strokes to clean the teeth?

How are you going to judge how clean the teeth are after the brushing?

## Tasting
How many different flavoured sweets can you get for 10p? Can you identify the flavour without seeing the sweet? Taste each kind of sweet and write a sentence describing its flavour.

Try putting a sweet in a blindfolded friend's mouth. Can he tell the flavour without sucking? Can he tell the flavour when sucking? Can he guess the colour? Try it with other children.

Buy a packet of fruit gums and place one sweet of each colour on a plate. Make a survey around the class to find each child's favourite amongst these. Is there a link between a child's favourite flavour and his favourite colour?

How many of the following can you identify by taste when blindfolded: carrot, turnip, swede, potato, cheese, apple, banana, grape, strawberry, pear, onion, coffee, tea, vinegar, fruit squashes, cube sugar, salt, chocolate?

Is it as easy if you hold your nose? (Why does food seem flavourless when you have a cold?) Is it easy to taste things after sucking an ice-cube?

Can you classify tastes into sweet, sour, salty and bitter? There are very few bitter tastes but try instant coffee and cooking chocolate. Some foods have a combination of flavours; sweet pickles, lemon drops and apples are both sweet and sour; peanut butter is sweet and salty.

Can you tell the difference between: sugar and saccharine; butter and margarine? (Try several kinds of each.)

How are you going to devise fair tests?

## Dilutions
Make up a solution of strong lime juice. Keep half. Halve the strength of the remainder by adding an equal amount of water. Keep half and halve the strength of the remainder. Continue doing this until you have a range of solutions.

How well do children fare in putting the solutions in order . . . by sight? . . . by taste?

# Legs and feet

Legs and feet vary in size—hence a good place to begin is with *measuring*.

## Measuring

### How long are your feet?
Place a centimetre ruler against the wall. Put your foot on top of the ruler with the heel touching the wall.

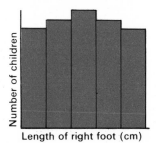

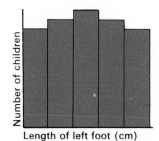

Write down the length of your foot to the nearest centimetre.

Is your right foot the same length as your left foot?

Measure the feet of other children in the class.

Measure the width of feet. Is the longest foot also the widest foot?

How many children have the first toe longer than the big toe?

## Another way to measure feet
Draw around the feet of several children on to a piece of paper—newspaper will do. Cut out the print. Arrange the cut-outs from the shortest to the longest and stick them on a long sheet of paper.

Can you tell from the chart which feet are flat and which are dented?

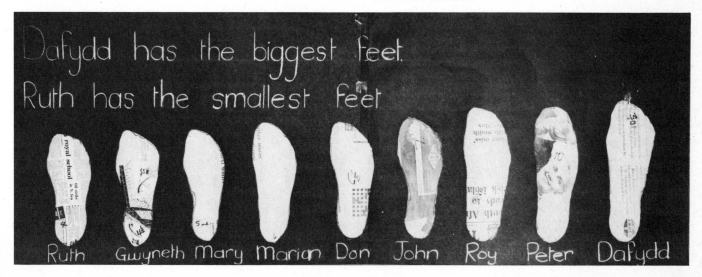

Dafydd has the biggest feet.
Ruth has the smallest feet

Ruth   Gwyneth   Mary   Marian   Don   John   Roy   Peter   Dafydd

## Measuring feet area

Draw around some feet on to centimetre-squared paper.

Find out the *area* of the left foot and the area of the right foot for a number of children by counting the squares. Ignore those squares which are less than half covered by the outline.

Is there a difference between right and left feet?

Is there any correlation between the area of a person's feet and their weight?

Work out the force exerted per square centimetre of foot.

Record the *shoe* area for each member of the group.

What force per square centimetre is exerted here?

How do girls compare with boys?

When Mum says 'my feet are killing me!' does she really put more pressure per square centimetre than Dad? Why did we have notices saying 'stiletto heels are banned'?

## Measuring legs

Measure the height of your knee above ground. Do this for other children. Is there a difference between boys and girls?

## Footprints

How can you find out if people's footprints are different? You might:

Paint a foot and press it on to a sheet of clean paper.

Stand a foot in talc and walk on black sugar paper.

Wet your feet and walk over paving stones.

Draw round a foot on to paper and cut around the outline print.

Can you think of other methods?

A good way to get very clear footprints is to put some paint on a large flat sponge, press the foot very lightly on the surface of the sponge and then press it on a sheet of clean white paper.

How many children have footprints like this?

How many children have footprints like this?

Which part of the foot touches the ground when you walk and which part touches the ground when you run?

How do prints obtained by running slowly compare with those obtained by running quickly?

## Toe prints

Paint the toes and the front part of the foot with powder paint. What sort of prints do you get when you are:

Standing flat on your foot?

Standing on your toes?

Crouching?

Springing forward?

Does this tell you anything about the use of the toes in body movement?

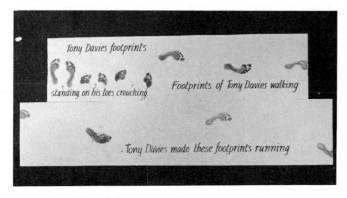

Tony Davies footprints

standing on his toes, crouching    Footprints of Tony Davies walking

Tony Davies made these footprints running

## A detective game

Form a small group of children—say six. One of the group, alone, must make various kinds of footprints outdoors. Can the rest of the group tell when he was walking?... when he was running?... when he was sitting down?

Footprints, tracks and trails left by other animals are worth noting too. If you are interested a book to help you is *Mammals of Britain, their Tracks, Trails and Signs* by Lawrence and Brown, published by Blandford.

## Feeling with the toes

Ask a willing subject to remove his shoes and socks. Blindfold him. Seat him as shown in the photograph.

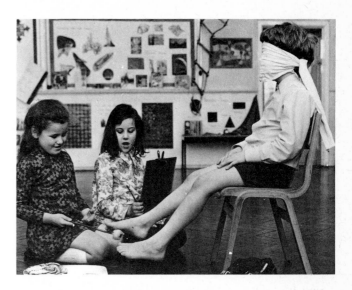

Can he identify a series of objects that you hold one at a time against his toes?

How good is he at distinguishing shapes?... textures? ... size? of objects.

How well can he distinguish the same objects felt by hand?

Can you tell what it is?

How do other children fare?

| Objects | Peter | | George | |
|---------|-------|---------|-------|---------|
| | Toes | Fingers | Toes | Fingers |
| a | | | | |
| b | | | | |
| c | | | | |

## Can you tell girls' feet from boys' feet?

Do boys' feet differ from girls' feet?

How could you devise a fair test?

## Leg power

### Jumping up

Some people can spring up higher into the air than others.

Try measuring this.

Stick some large sheets of white paper on to the wall with Sellotape.

Dab your fingers on to an ink-pad (a piece of blotting paper soaked with ink will do).

Stand alongside the sheets of paper with your heels flat on the ground and arm held as high as possible above your head.

Make a mark on the sheet with your inky fingers.

Leap as high as you possibly can up the wall and make a second mark.

Record the vertical distance between the two marks. Make records for a large number of children. Are boys better than girls at this?

Try making up a chart showing the average height of various age groups. Perhaps the plan below will help. You'll need to take a lot of results and sort them out to fit the categories listed in the tables. Even so time may allow results to be obtained from only one class.

|  | 7–8 years | 8–9 years | 9–10 years | 10–11 years |
|---|---|---|---|---|
| Excellent | $X$ cm |  |  |  |
| Very good |  |  |  |  |
| Good |  |  |  |  |
| Average |  |  |  |  |
| Fair |  |  |  |  |

$X$ cm = number of centimetres gained in leaping vertically upward.

## Jumping along
Who can do the furthest leap from a standing position?

Mark off a line outdoors on the grass or place some mats in the hall or a corridor to try this.

You can try making a table as before.

## Force exerted by the leg
Measure the *maximum* force exerted by the right foot pressing on a weighing scale. (It is best to use a scale calibrated in newtons. These are now available from most scientific suppliers.)

Place the scales upright against the wall. (Many scales have a hole in the base enabling them to be hung from a screw.)

Press against the scales whilst lying on the floor. This makes it difficult for anyone to put their weight on to the scale and one gets a truer measure of the force exerted.

Try with the left foot.

Is there a difference?

Get other children to try it. Are there any correlations to draw between force exerted and age, weight or sex?

## Force exerted by the knee

Repeat the experiment. This time press on the scales with the knee.

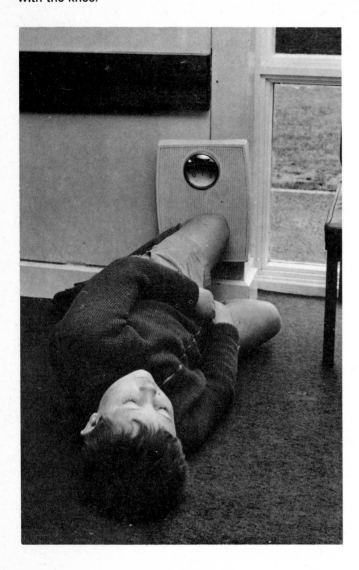

## Shoes and shoe care

It is useful when looking at feet to consider the shoes that go on them.

Why is the type of shoe above better than the type below?

Put some blocks under the heels of your shoes. What does raising the heels in this way do to the natural position of the body?

What effect will high heel shoes have?

Discuss the causes of bunions, corns and flat feet.

Have a friend draw round your foot (with shoe removed) on to a sheet of paper. Place your shoe carefully over the outline and draw round it.

Does your shoe fit properly?

# Arms and hands

## Measuring the length of fingers

Place your hand, palm downward, on a piece of paper. Draw round it to obtain an outline.

If you find it difficult to do hold your hand still and get someone else to draw around it.

How long is each finger?

Measure the fingers of other children in the same way. Make a careful record of your results.

Is finger number 2 always the longest?

Does anyone have some fingers the same length as one another?

What area does your hand cover?

What is the width of a hand-span?

Does the hand with the smallest hand-span cover the smallest area?

## Right thumb over left or left thumb over right?

Go around the class asking children to fold their hands *quickly*.

How many put their right thumb over their left thumb?

How many do it the other way round?

Is there any correlation between the way they fold their hands and being right- or left-handed?

## How big is your hand?

How many ways can you devise to measure the size of your hand? Here is one suggestion:

Obtain a tall, narrow jug. A clear plastic one is useful.

Put a suitable amount of water in and mark the side of the jug.

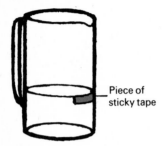

Piece of sticky tape

Put your right hand in up to the wrist and note how high the water rises.

Try it with the left hand. Is the left hand as big as the right hand?

Get other children to try it.

Don't forget to keep the jug topped up to the first fixed mark since some water will be lost each time on people's hands.

A variation on this method might be to stand the jug in a plastic bowl, fill it to the brim and measure the amount of water *displaced* by the hand.

Who has the biggest hand?

Who has the smallest hand?

Is your hand bigger if you open it out instead of keeping it as a fist?

## How much can your hand pick up?

Obtain a tin large enough to get your hand into comfortably with a bit over to spare. The large Nescafé tin used by caterers is a suitable size. Two-thirds fill it with seeds. Sunflower seeds are a good size to use. How many seeds can you pick up with your right hand?

It is best to have a container such as a plastic bowl that you can transfer your seeds into ready for counting.

Seeds

Counting so many seeds can be tedious. Try inventing some rapid ways of estimating the number of seeds you have taken. Measuring their volume or their weight might be useful suggestions for a start.

You might even have time to invent a simple balance to weigh the seeds.

Try your left hand. Does it pick up as many seeds as your right hand?

Find out how many seeds other children can pick up.

| BOYS | Left hand | Right hand | GIRLS | Left hand | Right hand |
|------|-----------|------------|-------|-----------|------------|
| Jim | Number of seeds | | Jane | | |
| John | | | Jean | | |

If there is time it would be useful to do this two or three times for each hand and then take the average.

Find out the hand in your class that picks up most seeds and compare it with the hand that picks up least. In which ways are the two hands different?

Is it just in size? Is it in length of fingers or what? Is the hand that picks up most seeds the biggest hand in the class?

Try marbles instead of seeds. Does the hand that picks up most seeds also pick up most marbles?

## How long is your forearm?

This is an exercise that calls for the greatest degree of accuracy. Measure with the help of a friend, the distance from your elbow to the tip of your middle finger. Use a long piece of string. Do at least two separate measurements. If they don't agree check with a third measurement. Is it different for right or left arm?

Try it for other children. Make a graph of length of forearm against age.

If you had a newcomer to your class could you predict the probable length of his forearm? Is there any correlation between length of forearm and height?

## Which muscles move the arm?

Bend and straighten your arm. Feel the muscles with the fingers of your free arm as you do this. Where are the muscles that bend the arm placed? Where are the muscles that straighten the arm?

Make a model from strong card to illustrate this.

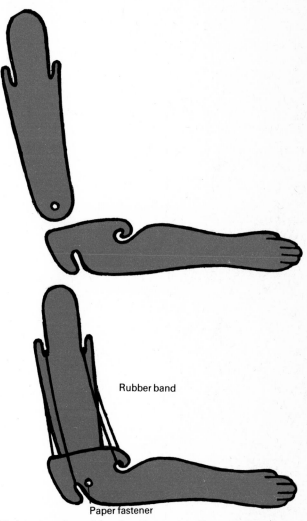

Rubber band

Paper fastener

Make sure the rubber bands are small enough to be stretched.

## How long can you hold up a stool?

The arm quickly gets fatigued when set an exercise.

Find out how long different children can hold up a stool.

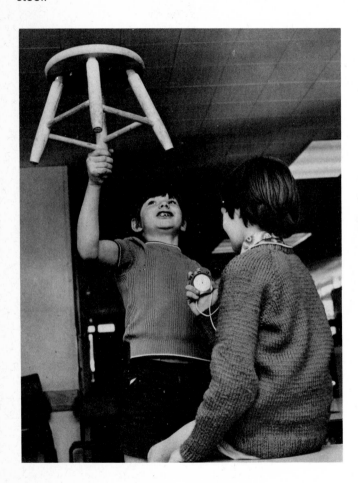

To make the test fair everyone should take up the same stance and hold the stool in the same way.

Can right hands hold the stool for a longer time than left hands?

How do left-handed children fare?

## How strong is a finger?

Use scales calibrated in newtons. Try pulling down on the scales with each of your fingers in turn.

How strong is each finger? How strong is the thumb?

Try it with other children.

Are the fingers of the right hand stronger than those of the left hand?

How do left-handed children fare?

# How strong is your grip?

How would you devise a method for testing this?

In one school the children began by hanging from a climbing frame.

Inevitably it was the smallest boy who could hang longest.

The children soon saw the unfairness of this test and one of them brought in a bent piece of wrought iron.

It was possible to squeeze this inward with the hand.

How were they to measure how much they could do this?

They found an easy solution was to squeeze the bar and quickly dab it on to a block of Plasticine.

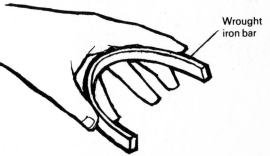

Wrought iron bar

It was then very simple to measure between the marks that had been made.

An even simpler method was to mark the tips of the horseshoe-shaped bar with ink, press it inward and dab it on to a sheet of paper.

One group of boys became really interested, and with the teacher's help made up this grip tester.

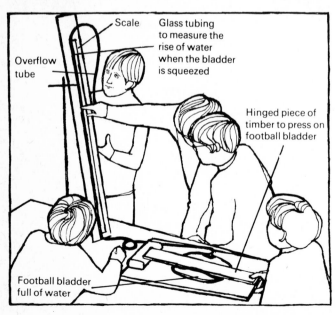

Scale

Glass tubing to measure the rise of water when the bladder is squeezed

Overflow tube

Hinged piece of timber to press on football bladder

Football bladder full of water

Here is a further suggestion.

Clear, plastic tubing can be obtained from any scientific suppliers and can very often be got from a local garage.

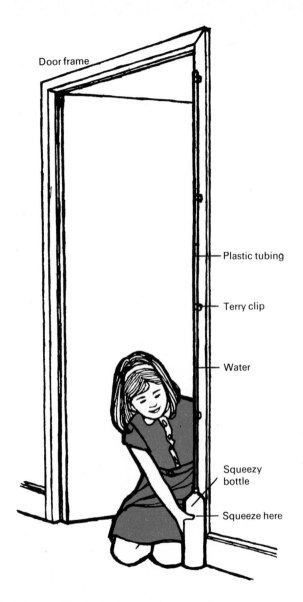

Door frame

Plastic tubing

Terry clip

Water

Squeezy bottle

Squeeze here

Another method, that older juniors with a wide enough stretch of their fingers can try, is to grip across bathroom scales calibrated in newtons.

## Fingerprints

It has never been known for two people to possess identical fingerprints. Even identical twins have slightly different prints.

All prints are of one of four types:

Whorl       Loop

Arch       Composite

All or only one of these forms may occur on the fingers of both hands.

It is very easy to take a fingerprint but more difficult to get a clear, worthwhile print. It has to be done very carefully.

Use an ink pad or a folded sheet of blotting paper soaked with ink. Roll your finger on the inked surface. Press this inked finger from side to side, *once* on a piece of paper. You'll have to experiment several times until you get just the right amount of ink on your finger to make a good print. Don't press too hard!

Is the fingerprint of your first finger the same on both hands?

Is the fingerprint of your index finger the same as the fingerprint of the index finger of other people?

Are all your fingerprints the same?

A fingerprint made on a glass slide can often be effectively projected on a screen using a slide projector.

## A detective game

Cover a book with a sheet of plain white paper.

Take the fingerprints of four of your friends.

Ink their fingers and tell them that one of them must pick up the books whilst you are out of the room.

Can you tell from the prints left on the book which of your friends did so?

Sir Harold Scott in his book *Scotland Yard* published by Penguin has a useful chapter on fingerprints. Here he notes that of the impressions taken by Scotland Yard roughly sixty per cent are loops, five per cent are arches, thirty-five per cent whorls and composites.

## Feeling with the fingers

How does the sense of touch vary between different children?

Blindfolded children can examine a range of objects by feeling, lifting and handling them generally.

It is useful to have a companion to note down their observations. (Don't forget useful records can be made with a tape-recorder.)

What texture, shape, size, weight are the objects?

Do they feel warm or cold?

Are they in more than one piece?

Are any of them fragile?

## Different surfaces

Feelings can be confined to one aspect such as the surface of objects. Can you distinguish between sandpaper, glass paper, blotting paper, writing paper, rubber sheeting, plastic, tissue paper, velvet, wood, satin, wool, linen and so on? Present each of these in turn to blindfolded friends. Present some of them several times and see if you can catch your friends out.

Make a record of your results.

Do you get the same results if you try these surfaces against the toes, the knee or the forehead?

It is also useful to obtain a range of cards of different thicknesses. Can you sort these into groups or order when blindfolded?

## How well can your hands judge temperature?

Put one of your hands in cold water (plus ice if available) and the other hand in hot water as shown below:

Ice-cold water          Lukewarm water          Hot water

Now transfer both hands to the bowl of lukewarm water.

How does each hand feel?

42

# Some games and us

## Catching

Ask a friend to try making ten consecutive catches with the right hand, ten consecutive catches with the left and and ten consecutive catches with both hands.

Record the results.

Try a number of people—boys, girls, adults.

Are boys better than girls?

Does being right- or left-handed have an effect?

Are younger people better than older people?

## Hop, skip and jump

Gather a group of friends and mark off a starting line. Each person in turn does a hop, a skip and a jump. Measure the distance.

Measure each person's height as well. Is there any relationship between height and the distance covered in the hop, skip and jump?

## Aiming at a skittle

Try aiming at a skittle with a small ball from 20 m, . . . 10 m, . . . 5 m.

How successful are you at each distance? Do you improve with practice?

## Heading a ball

How many times can you head a football between yourself and a partner? Have ten attempts. Do you improve?

## Throwing bean bags

Take ten bean bags and stand ten paces from a bucket. Toss the bean bags into the bucket. How successful were you?

Move a pace nearer the bucket and throw the bean bag again. Repeat from seven, six, five paces away. Do you improve as you get nearer?

Which factors are most important—practice or distance?

## Skipping

Try skipping in as many different ways as you know: forward, backward, double bounce and so on.

How many skips can you keep up for each style?

Which is the most difficult? Is it the same for everyone?

## Judging length

Blindfold a friend. Ask him to feel the length of an object such as a book or satchel placed in front of him. Then tell him to put his hands together. Now ask him to extend his hands to the length of the original object. How good an estimate does he make?

How good is he with a range of objects?

Does he get better with practice?

## Dribbling

How well can you dribble a ball in and out of a series of markers?

How long does it take?

Can you speed up with practice?

What happens if you try it in the reverse direction? ... redistribute the markers?

## Shadows

Shadow games, like jumping on your shadow, are good at helping young children develop their awareness of space and learn about the properties of shadows. This aspect is more fully explored in the Unit *Early experiences.*

# Memory

Most of us have difficulty in remembering numbers. Telephone numbers for example. Get someone to read out the figures below *one line at a time.*

247812
3749172
53712135
616731579
7903175293

Try repeating the numbers in the order given. How well do members of the class fare in this test?

Try the same thing with letters:

s t y w
p q r a c
m l d t p z
t e i h b n r
n r s o l m f l
h z l g s y j k p

Are your friends better at remembering letters than numbers? What about words?

Try: tray gorse bed
      man clock desk whistle
      pen glove shoe nail rubber
      paper elephant leaf glass bell hat
      fruit head car door tin jar flower
      snow bald match cup house pencil cat box

Are you better at remembering words when they are strung together as sentences? Copy out a number of sentences from a book. Find sentences varying in length from ten to thirty words. Put them in order of number of words.

Read out the shortest sentence and ask a friend to repeat it. Try a slightly longer sentence. How does your friend cope as the sentences get longer and longer?

## A memory game
Show a tray holding a variety of objects to a small group of friends for one minute. How many objects can they remember when the tray is removed? Do they improve with practice?

# How quick are you?

How quickly do you react in certain situations? What about your friends? Why should it be important for us to have a quick *reaction time*?

Try to investigate how quickly your friends react.

## Catching a marked card

Mark a stout piece of card about 30 cm long and 2 cm wide at 2-cm intervals.

Choose a partner to stand with finger and thumb flanking the card as shown in the diagram.

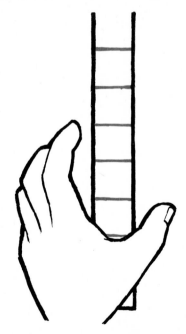

At what mark can your partner catch it when you let it

go? Does his performance improve with practice? Try other people. Make a graph of your results.

## Dropping a pebble

Drop a pebble from the 25-cm mark on your ruler.

Can your partner remove his hand before the pebble hits it?

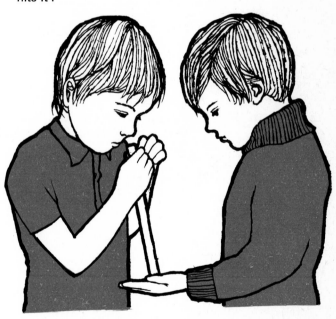

If he is successful try it from a lower mark. Is he successful this time?

How near to his hand can you drop the pebble before he is unsuccessful? Try it with the foot and measure foot reaction time.

# A group reaction

Here a group of people can time the interval between receiving some stimulus and acting upon it.

Let the whole class of children stand in a circle, holding hands. One child holds the stop-watch and acts as leader.

Stop-watch

The child on his right holds his arm instead of his hand. As the leader starts the watch he squeezes the hand of the person on his left. This child passes the squeeze on to the next child and so on around the circle, the leader stopping the watch as soon as the squeeze returns to him.

Repeat the game several times doing it both ways round the circle. Take the average time and divide by the number of children in order to get the average individual reaction time.

Is it best to face inward or outward?

What other factors affect the group reaction time?

What is the effect on the group reaction time of removing individuals from the circle?

A variation on this method is to stand children in a line about 60 cm apart. One child touches the back of the child in front of him who in turn touches the child ahead of him and so on down the line.

Stop-watch

The child who begins the sequence starts a stop-watch as he touches the person in front of him. He stops the watch as soon as the child at the head of the line calls out.

There are lots of conditions under which to do these tests.

Do you get the same results first thing in the morning and last thing in the afternoon?

Do you get the same results three weeks later? Is there any link between time taken and age, sex or time of getting up?

# Body activities

Breathing and pulse rate and their interrelationship makes a fairly easy area for exploration by older juniors.

## How big is your chest? How much bigger can you make it?

Measure the chest size with a piece of string. Breathe out until the lungs are emptied of air. Measure the chest.

Breathe in until the lungs are fully expanded. Measure the chest.

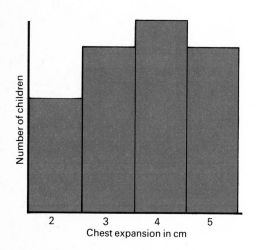

How much chest expansion do you have?

How much chest expansion does each of your friends have?

## Is there a link between chest size and air capacity of the lungs?

Fill a large plastic container with water. The sort of semi-transparent container used for holding water when camping is ideal. Invert the full container into a sink or large bowl. Insert a piece of rubber tubing through the neck.

Breathe in deeply, expand the chest to its full extent and breathe out through the tube. The expelled air will displace water from the plastic container giving a measure of how much air is breathed out.

Pinch the tube shut as soon as you finish breathing out.

How much air did you breathe out?

How much air can other children breathe out?

Is there a link between chest expansion and amount of air expelled?

| Chest expansion in cm | Amount of air expelled | Average |
|---|---|---|
| 2 | John<br>Sally<br>Wendy | |
| 3 | Peter<br>Roy<br>James<br>Martin | |
| 4 | Sheila<br>Lucy<br>Paul<br>Oliver | |
| 5 | Jane<br>Michael | |

## The pulse and breathing

### Pulse rate
Find your pulse with the index finger. Count how many beats there are per minute. Do this three separate times and take the average.

Who has the highest pulse rate in the class?

Who has the lowest pulse rate in the class?

Do girls differ from boys?

Pulse rates differ with age so try and get records from members of the school staff as well as from children in the class. Young children have a high pulse rate, records from two- and three-year-olds will be interesting.

### Rate of breathing
Count the number of breaths you take in one minute. Do this three times and take the average.

Is there any relationship between pulse rate and breathing? Run around the playground and take your pulse rate. How has it changed? What about your breathing rate: has that changed?

# Other things to do

## Other activities

There are many other activities that link closely with the topic of 'Ourselves'.

### Statistics
Firstly, there are lots of statistics that can be collected, collated and sometimes graphed.

How many boys are there?

How many girls are there?

How many stay for school dinner?

How many brothers and sisters does each child have?

How much time does each child spend watching television? What is the class average?

How many pets do children in the class possess?

How many ways can these pets be classified?

### Looking after ourselves
Secondly, there is the problem of looking after ourselves.

How do we keep warm?

What do we wear?

How does the clothing we wear differ in warm and cold weather?

Which materials are best for losing heat?

What properties do cotton and linen have that make them ideal for summer wear?

Is colour of clothing important?

What clothes do people wear in other lands?

How do we keep our homes warm?

How much do we eat and drink in a day? How much have we eaten in our lives?

What can we find out about foods and diet?

How do we cook our food?

How do we keep ourselves clean?

What do we do to ensure general hygiene?

How many different ways can we communicate with one another?

### Likes and dislikes
Thirdly, there are our likes and dislikes.

What are our favourite colours?

What do we like to eat, to drink, to read, to watch on television or listen to on the radio?

### Man's discoveries
Fourthly, there is the history of man's discoveries about himself.

Look at Leonardo da Vinci's drawings of the body.

Read the story of Harvey's discovery of the circulation

of the blood.

Find out about Pasteur's and Lister's work on bacteria and antiseptics.

## Odds and ends
Finally, there are a host of odds and ends that might interest children.

What does being alive mean?

When do birthdays occur?

Can children link any famous events with their birthdays?

Which signs of the Zodiac do they come under?

What is a horoscope?

What do their parents do?

What hair styles are there among the children?

What fashions? Look at fashions through the ages.

What does everyone in the class do on Sunday?

Invent a family or a class 'coat of arms'.

# Objectives for children learning science
## Guide lines to keep in mind

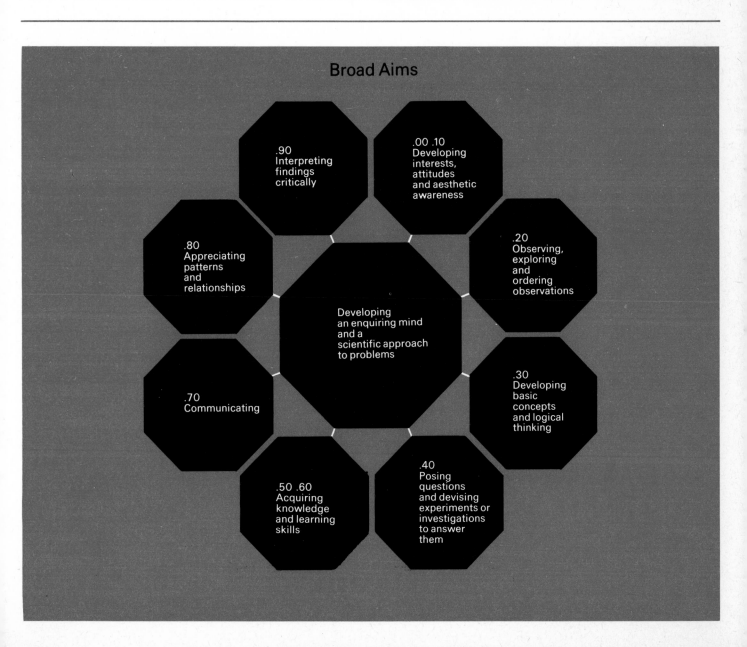

Broad Aims

.90
Interpreting
findings
critically

.00 .10
Developing
interests,
attitudes
and aesthetic
awareness

.80
Appreciating
patterns
and
relationships

.20
Observing,
exploring
and
ordering
observations

Developing
an enquiring mind
and a
scientific approach
to problems

.70
Communicating

.30
Developing
basic
concepts
and logical
thinking

.50 .60
Acquiring
knowledge
and learning
skills

.40
Posing
questions
and devising
experiments or
investigations
to answer
them

# What we mean by Stage 1, Stage 2 and Stage 3

# Attitudes, interests and aesthetic awareness

## .00/.10

**Stage 1**
Transition from intuition to concrete operations. Infants generally.

The characteristics of thought among infant children differ in important respects from those of children over the age of about seven years. Infant thought has been described as 'intuitive' by Piaget; it is closely associated with physical action and is dominated by immediate observation. Generally, the infant is not able to think about or imagine the consequences of an action unless he has actually carried it out, nor is he yet likely to draw logical conclusions from his experiences. At this early stage the objectives are those concerned with active exploration of the immediate environment and the development of ability to discuss and communicate effectively: they relate to the kind of activities that are appropriate to these very young children, and which form an introduction to ways of exploring and of ordering observations.

1.01 Willingness to ask questions
1.02 Willingness to handle both living and non-living material.
1.03 Sensitivity to the need for giving proper care to living things.
1.04 Enjoyment in using all the senses for exploring and discriminating.
1.05 Willingness to collect material for observation or investigation.

---

Concrete operations. Early stage.

In this Stage, children are developing the ability to manipulate things mentally. At first this ability is limited to objects and materials that can be manipulated concretely, and even then only in a restricted way. The objectives here are concerned with developing these mental operations through exploration of concrete objects and materials—that is to say, objects and materials which, as physical things, have meaning for the child. Since older children, and even adults prefer an introduction to new ideas and problems through concrete example and physical exploration, these objectives are suitable for all children, whatever their age, who are being introduced to certain science activities for the first time.

1.06 Desire to find out things for oneself.
1.07 Willing participation in group work.
1.08 Willing compliance with safety regulations in handling tools and equipment.
1.09 Appreciation of the need to learn the meaning of new words and to use them correctly.

**Stage 2**
Concrete operations. Later stage.

In this Stage, a continuation of what Piaget calls the stage of concrete operations, the mental manipulations are becoming more varied and powerful. The developing ability to handle variables—for example, in dealing with multiple classification—means that problems can be solved in more ordered and quantitative ways than was previously possible. The objectives begin to be more specific to the exploration of the scientific aspects of the environment rather than to general experience, as previously. These objectives are developments of those of Stage 1 and depend on them for a foundation. They are those thought of as being appropriate for all children who have progressed from Stage 1 and not merely for nine- to eleven-year-olds.

2.01 Willingness to co-operate with others in science activities.
2.02 Willingness to observe objectively.
2.03 Appreciation of the reasons for safety regulations.
2.04 Enjoyment in examining ambiguity in the use of words.
2.05 Interest in choosing suitable means of expressing results and observations.
2.06 Willingness to assume responsibility for the proper care of living things.
2.07 Willingness to examine critically the results of their own and others' work.
2.08 Preference for putting ideas to test before accepting or rejecting them.
2.09 Appreciation that approximate methods of comparison may be more appropriate than careful measurements.

**Stage 3**
Transition to stage of abstract thinking.

This is the Stage in which, for some children, the ability to think about abstractions is developing. When this development is complete their thought is capable of dealing with the possible and hypothetical, and is not tied to the concrete and to the here and now. It may take place between eleven and thirteen for some able children, for some children it may happen later, and for others it may never occur. The objectives of this stage are ones which involve development of ability to use hypothetical reasoning and to separate and combine variables in a systematic way. They are appropriate to those who have achieved most of the Stage 2 objectives and who now show signs of ability to manipulate mentally ideas and propositions.

3.01 Acceptance of responsibility for their own and others' safety in experiments.
3.02 Preference for using words correctly.
3.03 Commitment to the idea of physical cause and effect.
3.04 Recognition of the need to standardise measurements.
3.05 Willingness to examine evidence critically.
3.06 Willingness to consider beforehand the usefulness of the results from a possible experiment.
3.07 Preference for choosing the most appropriate means of expressing results or observations.
3.08 Recognition of the need to acquire new skills.
3.09 Willingness to consider the role of science in everyday life.

## Attitudes, interests and aesthetic awareness

### .00/.10

## Observing, exploring and ordering observations

### .20

| |
|---|
| 1.21 Appreciation of the variety of living things and materials in the environment. |
| 1.22 Awareness of changes which take place as time passes. |
| 1.23 Recognition of common shapes—square, circle, triangle. |
| 1.24 Recognition of regularity in patterns. |
| 1.25 Ability to group things consistently according to chosen or given criteria. |

1.11 Awareness that there are various ways of testing out ideas and making observations.

1.12 Interest in comparing and classifying living or non-living things.

1.13 Enjoyment in comparing measurements with estimates.

1.14 Awareness that there are various ways of expressing results and observations.

1.15 Willingness to wait and to keep records in order to observe change in things.

1.16 Enjoyment in exploring the variety of living things in the environment.

1.17 Interest in discussing and comparing the aesthetic qualities of materials.

1.26 Awareness of the structure and form of living things.

1.27 Awareness of change of living things and non-living materials.

1.28 Recognition of the action of force

1.29 Ability to group living and non-living things by observable attributes.

1.29a Ability to distinguish regularity in events and motion.

2.11 Enjoyment in developing methods for solving problems or testing ideas.

2.12 Appreciation of the part that aesthetic qualities of materials play in determining their use.

2.13 Interest in the way discoveries were made in the past.

2.21 Awareness of internal structure in living and non-living things.

2.22 Ability to construct and use keys for identification.

2.23 Recognition of similar and congruent shapes.

2.24 Awareness of symmetry in shapes and structures.

2.25 Ability to classify living things and non-living materials in different ways.

2.26 Ability to visualise objects from different angles and the shape of cross-sections.

3.11 Appreciation of the main principles in the care of living things.

3.12 Willingness to extend methods used in science activities to other fields of experience.

3.21 Appreciation that classification criteria are arbitrary.

3.22 Ability to distinguish observations which are relevant to the solution of a problem from those which are not.

3.23 Ability to estimate the order of magnitude of physical quantities.

|  | **Developing basic concepts and logical thinking** .30 | **Posing questions and devising experiments or investigations to answer them** .40 |
|---|---|---|
| **Stage 1** Transition from intuition to concrete operations. Infants generally. | *1.31* Awareness of the meaning of words which describe various types of quantity. <br> *1.32* Appreciation that things which are different may have features in common. | *1.41* Ability to find answers to simple problems by investigation <br> *1.42* Ability to make comparisons in terms of one property or variable. |
| Concrete operations. Early stage. | *1.33* Ability to predict the effect of certain changes through observation of similar changes. <br> *1.34* Formation of the notions of the horizontal and the vertical. <br> *1.35* Development of concepts of conservation of length and substance. <br> *1.36* Awareness of the meaning of speed and of its relation to distance covered. | *1.43* Appreciation of the need for measurement. <br> *1.44* Awareness that more than one variable may be involved in a particular change. |
| **Stage 2** Concrete operations. Later stage. | *2.31* Appreciation of measurement as division into regular parts and repeated comparison with a unit. <br> *2.32* Appreciation that comparisons can be made indirectly by use of an intermediary. <br> *2.33* Development of concepts of conservation of weight, area and volume. <br> *2.34* Appreciation of weight as a downward force. <br> *2.35* Understanding of the speed, time, distance relation. | *2.41* Ability to frame questions likely to be answered through investigations. <br> *2.42* Ability to investigate variables and to discover effective ones. <br> *2.43* Appreciation of the need to control variables and use controls in investigations. <br> *2.44* Ability to choose and use either arbitrary or standard units of measurement as appropriate. <br> *2.45* Ability to select a suitable degree of approximation and work to it. <br> *2.46* Ability to use representational models for investigating problems or relationships. |
| **Stage 3** Transition to stage of abstract thinking. | *3.31* Familiarity with relationships involving velocity, distance, time, acceleration. <br> *3.32* Ability to separate, exclude or combine variables in approaching problems. <br> *3.33* Ability to formulate hypotheses not dependent upon direct observation. <br> *3.34* Ability to extend reasoning beyond the actual to the possible. <br> *3.35* Ability to distinguish a logically sound proof from others less sound. | *3.41* Attempting to identify the essential steps in approaching a problem scientifically. <br> *3.42* Ability to design experiments with effective controls for testing hypotheses. <br> *3.43* Ability to visualise a hypothetical situation as a useful simplification of actual observations. <br> *3.44* Ability to construct scale models for investigation and to appreciate implications of changing the scale. |

*1.51* Ability to discriminate between different materials.
*1.52* Awareness of the characteristics of living things.
*1.53* Awareness of properties which materials can have.
*1.54* Ability to use displayed reference material for identifying living and non-living things.

- - - - - - - - - - - - - - - - - - - - - - - - - - - - - - - -

*1.55* Familiarity with sources of sound.
*1.56* Awareness of sources of heat, light and electricity.
*1.57* Knowledge that change can be produced in common substances.
*1.58* Appreciation that ability to move or cause movement requires energy.
*1.59* Knowledge of differences in properties between and within common groups of materials.

*1.61* Appreciation of man's use of other living things and their products.
*1.62* Awareness that man's way of life has changed through the ages.
*1.63* Skill in manipulating tools and materials.
*1.64* Development of techniques for handling living things correctly.
*1.65* Ability to use books for supplementing ideas or information.

*2.51* Knowledge of conditions which promote changes in living things and non-living materials.
*2.52* Familiarity with a wide range of forces and of ways in which they can be changed.
*2.53* Knowledge of sources and simple properties of common forms of energy.
*2.54* Knowledge of the origins of common materials.
*2.55* Awareness of some discoveries and inventions by famous scientists.
*2.56* Knowledge of ways to investigate and measure properties of living things and non-living materials.
*2.57* Awareness of changes in the design of measuring instruments and tools during man's history.
*2.58* Skill in devising and constructing simple apparatus.
*2.59* Ability to select relevant information from books or other reference material.

*3.51* Knowledge that chemical change results from interaction.
*3.52* Knowledge that energy can be stored and converted in various ways.
*3.53* Awareness of the universal nature of gravity.
*3.54* Knowledge of the main constituents and variations in the composition of soil and of the earth.
*3.55* Knowledge that properties of matter can be explained by reference to its particulate nature.
*3.56* Knowledge of certain properties of heat, light, sound, electrical, mechanical and chemical energy.
*3.57* Knowledge of a wide range of living organisms.
*3.58* Development of the concept of an internal environment.
*3.59* Knowledge of the nature and variations in basic life processes.

*3.61* Appreciation of levels of organisation in living things.
*3.62* Appreciation of the significance of the work and ideas of some famous scientists.
*3.63* Ability to apply relevant knowledge without help of contextual cues.
*3.64* Ability to use scientific equipment and instruments for extending the range of human senses.

|  | **Communicating** | **Appreciating patterns and relationships** |
|---|---|---|
|  | **.70** | **.80** |

**Stage 1**
Transition from
intuition to
concrete
operations.
Infants
generally.

*1.71* Ability to use new words appropriately.
*1.72* Ability to record events in their sequences.
*1.73* Ability to discuss and record impressions of living and non-living things in the environment.
*1.74* Ability to use representational symbols for recording information on charts or block graphs.

*1.81* Awareness of cause-effect relationships.

- - - - - - - - - - - - - - - - - - - - - - - - - - - - - - - - - - - - - - - - - - - - - -

Concrete
operations.
Early stage.

*1.75* Ability to tabulate information and use tables.
*1.76* Familiarity with names of living things and non-living materials.
*1.77* Ability to record impressions by making models, painting or drawing.

*1.82* Development of a concept of environment.
*1.83* Formation of a broad idea of variation in living things.
*1.84* Awareness of seasonal changes in living things.
*1.85* Awareness of differences in physical conditions between different parts of the Earth.

**Stage 2**
Concrete
operations.
Later stage.

*2.71* Ability to use non-representational symbols in plans, charts, etc.
*2.72* Ability to interpret observations in terms of trends and rates of change.
*2.73* Ability to use histograms and other simple graphical forms for communicating data.
*2.74* Ability to construct models as a means of recording observations.

*2.81* Awareness of sequences of change in natural phenomena.
*2.82* Awareness of structure-function relationship in parts of living things.
*2.83* Appreciation of interdependence among living things.
*2.84* Awareness of the impact of man's activities on other living things.
*2.85* Awareness of the changes in the physical environment brought about by man's activity.
*2.86* Appreciation of the relationships of parts and wholes.

**Stage 3**
Transition to
stage of
abstract
thinking.

*3.71* Ability to select the graphical form most appropriate to the information being recorded.
*3.72* Ability to use three-dimensional models or graphs for recording results.
*3.73* Ability to deduce information from graphs: from gradient, area, intercept.
*3.74* Ability to use analogies to explain scientific ideas and theories.

*3.81* Recognition that the ratio of volume to surface area is significant.
*3.82* Appreciation of the scale of the universe.
*3.83* Understanding of the nature and significance of changes in living and non-living things.
*3.84* Recognition that energy has many forms and is conserved when it is changed from one form to another.
*3.85* Recognition of man's impact on living things— conservation, change, control.
*3.86* Appreciation of the social implications of man's changing use of materials, historical and contemporary.
*3.87* Appreciation of the social implications of research in science.
*3.88* Appreciation of the role of science in the changing pattern of provision for human needs.

## Interpreting findings critically

### .90

*1.91* Awareness that the apparent size, shape and relationships of things depend on the position of the observer.

---

*1.92* Appreciation that properties of materials influence their use.

---

*2.91* Appreciation of adaptation to environment.
*2.92* Appreciation of how the form and structure of materials relate to their function and properties.
*2.93* Awareness that many factors need to be considered when choosing a material for a particular use.
*2.94* Recognition of the role of chance in making measurements and experiments.

These Stages we have chosen conform to modern ideas about children's learning. They conveniently describe for us the mental development of children between the ages of five and thirteen years, but it must be remembered that ALTHOUGH CHILDREN GO THROUGH THESE STAGES IN THE SAME ORDER THEY DO NOT GO THROUGH THEM AT THE SAME RATES.
SOME children achieve the later Stages at an early age.
SOME loiter in the early Stages for quite a time.
SOME never have the mental ability to develop to the later Stages.
ALL appear to be ragged in their movement from one Stage to another.
Our Stages, then, are not tied to chronological age, so in any one class of children there will be, almost certainly, some children at differing Stages of mental development.

---

*3.91* Ability to draw from observations conclusions that are unbiased by preconception.
*3.92* Willingness to accept factual evidence despite perceptual contradictions.
*3.93* Awareness that the degree of accuracy of measurements has to be taken into account when results are interpreted.
*3.94* Awareness that unstated assumptions can affect conclusions drawn from argument or experimental results.
*3.95* Appreciation of the need to integrate findings into a simplifying generalisation.
*3.96* Willingness to check that conclusions are consistent with further evidence.

# Index

**Illustration acknowledgements:**

The publishers gratefully acknowledge the help given by the following in supplying photographs on the pages indicated:

James Wright. 6, 10 bottom, 12, 14, 18
South West Picture Agency Limited, all other photographs

Line drawings by The Garden Studio: Anna Barnard

Flow charts and labelling by GWA Design Consultants Ltd

Cover design by Peter Gauld